A Teaching Guide to

My Side of the Mountain

by Mary F. Spicer

Illustration by Kathy Kifer and Dahna Solar

Dedicated to
Wendel Z. (Sam) Hall
1938-1994
A teacher's teacher—always a source of inspiration
and encouragement to me.

My Side of the Mountain
Puffin Books
Published by the Penguin Group
Viking Penguin, a Division of Penguin Books USA Inc.,
New York, New York 10014

Published by:
Garlic Press
605 Powers St.
Eugene, OR 97402

ISBN 0-931993-76-8
Order Number GP-076

www.garlicpress.com

Table of Contents

The Discovering Literature Series is designed to develop a student's appreciation for good literature and to improve reading comprehension. While many skills reinforce a student's ability to comprehend what he or she reads (sequencing, cause and effect, finding details, using context clues), two skills are vital. They are: discerning **main ideas** and **summarizing** text. Students who can master these two essential skills develop into sophisticated readers.

The following discussion details the various elements that constitute this Series.

About Chapter Organization

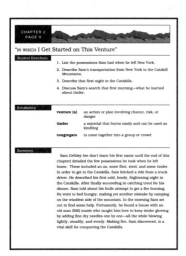

Sample: Chapter 2 with Student Directives, Chapter Vocabulary, and Chapter Summary.

Each chapter analysis is organized into three basic elements: **Student Directives**, **Chapter Vocabulary**, and **Chapter Summary**. Student Directives and Chapter Vocabulary need to be displayed on the board or on an overhead projector after each chapter is read. Students copy the Chapter Vocabulary and write their own summaries following the Student Directives.

The **Student Directives** contain the main ideas in each chapter. They provide the students, working individually or in groups, with a framework for developing their summaries. Student Directives can also be used as group discussion topics.

The **Chapter Vocabulary** includes definitions of key words from each chapter. To save time, students need only to copy, not look up, definitions. Suggestions for teaching vocabulary to students are as follows:

1. Make and display flashcards with the words and definitions. Refer to vocabulary cards in daily review.
2. Have students write sentences individually, in groups, or as a class using the words in the story's context.
3. Give frequent quizzes before an actual test.
4. Have students make their own vocabulary crossword puzzles or word search puzzles.
5. Play 20 questions with vocabulary words.
6. Host a vocabulary bee where the students give definitions for the word rather than spelling it.

A **Chapter Summary** for each chapter is included for teacher use and knowledge. Some students may initially need to copy the summaries in order to feel comfortable writing their own subsequent ones. Other students can use the completed summaries as a comparison to guide their own work. Summary

Sample:
Blackline Master

writing provides an opportunity to polish student composition skills, in addition to reading skills.

The **blackline master**, *Chapter Summary & Vocabulary*, is provided on page 67. It can be duplicated for student use. Teachers can also use it to make transparencies for displaying Student Directives and Chapter Vocabulary.

In addition, teachers may opt to have students make folders to house their Chapter Summary & Vocabulary sheets. A sample cover sheet (see page 68) for student embellishments has been provided. Cover sheets can be laminated, if desired, and affixed to a manila (or other) folder.

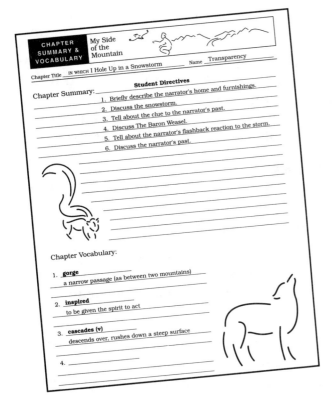

Sample Transparency:
Student Directives and Chapter Vocabulary

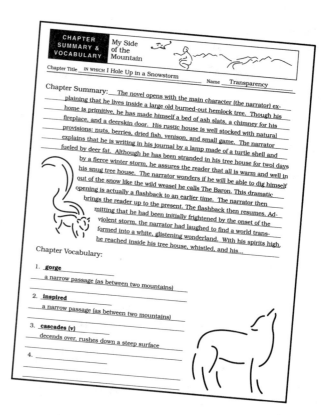

Sample Transparency:
Chapter Summary and Chapter Vocabulary

The above two samples serve to illustrate how the **blackline master**, *Chapter Summary & Vocabulary*, can be used as a transparency to focus student work. These transparencies are particularly effective for displaying Student Directives and Chapter Vocabulary. They are also effective for initially modeling how Chapter Summaries can be written.

Sample: Skill Page

Skill Pages throughout the series have been developed to increase students' understanding of various literary elements and to reinforce vital reading skills. Since the entire series is devoted to reinforcing **main ideas** and **summarizing** skills, no further work has been provided on these skills. Depending upon each novel, Skill Pages reinforce various skills from among the following: **outlining**; **cause and effect**; **sequencing**; **character**, **setting**, **and plot development**; and **figurative language**. You will note that character development is based upon a values framework.

About the
Tests

Sample: Test

At the end of each five-chapter block, a comprehensive open-book **Test** has been developed for your use. Each test includes reading comprehension, vocabulary, and short essays.

An Answer Key is provided at the back of the book for each Test.

The vocabulary portion of the Tests may be particularly difficult. You will probably want to give one or two vocabulary quizzes before administering each of the four Tests.

About the
Writer's Forum

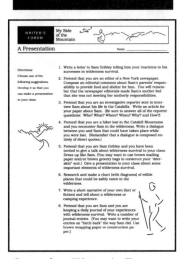

Sample: Writer's Forum

Suggestions for writing are presented under the **Writer's Forum** throughout this guide. You can choose from these suggestions or substitute your own creative-writing ideas.

"IN WHICH I Hole Up in a Snowstorm"

About Chapter 1

Chapter 1 of *My Side of the Mountain* is often difficult for students because of the author's use of the flashback technique. As such, you may choose to introduce *My Side of the Mountain* with the standard Chapter Summary & Vocabulary sheet (see page 67), with the Flashback Development exercise (see page 10), or with both.

Student Directives

1. Briefly describe the narrator's home and furnishings.

2. Discuss the snowstorm.

3. Tell about the clue to the narrator's past.

4. Discuss The Baron Weasel.

5. Tell about the narrator's flashback reaction to the storm.

6. Discuss the narrator's past.

Vocabulary

gorge	a narrow passage (as between two mountains)
inspired	to be given the spirit to act
cascades (v)	descends over, rushes down a steep surface

Summary

The novel opens with the main character (the narrator) explaining that he lives inside a large old burned-out hemlock tree. Though his home is primitive, he has made himself a bed of ash slats, a chimney for his fireplace, and a deerskin door. His rustic house is well stocked with natural provisions: nuts, berries, dried fish, venison, and small game. The narrator explains that he is writing in his journal by a lamp made of a turtle shell and fueled by deer fat. Although he has been stranded in his tree house for two days by a fierce winter storm, he assures the reader that all is warm and well in his snug tree house. The narrator wonders if he will be able to dig himself out of the snow like the wild weasel he calls The Baron. This dramatic opening is actually a flashback to an earlier time. The narrator then brings

"IN WHICH I Hole Up in a Snowstorm," Page 2

the reader up to the present. The flashback then resumes. Admitting that he had been initially frightened by the onset of the violent storm, the narrator had laughed to find a world transformed into a white, glistening wonderland. With his spirits high, he reached inside his tree house, whistled, and his trained falcon, Frightful, flew to his fist. The narrator then explains that he had decided to live off the land in the Catskill Mountains because he had shared a crowded New York City apartment with ten other family members. The young man (whose family name is Gribley) had wanted some land to call his own—land he remembered from his father's stories about Great-grandfather Gribley's farm.

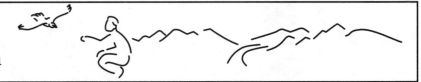
Flashback Development

The author, Jean Craighead George, uses the flashback technique to introduce readers to *My Side of the Mountain*. This technique is an introductory device sometimes used by scriptwriters. Flashbacks allow the author to open a narrative with a "dramatic event" that captures the reader's imagination and compels her or him to read further.

A flashback is a scene representing an earlier event that is inserted into a current situation depicted in a novel, motion picture, play, etc.

The following exercise may be substituted for the normal Chapter Summary and Vocabulary. This flashback exercise will help to bring the first chapter into better focus for your students. It will help to order and arrange events and surroundings which otherwise may seem scattered or unrelated. Ordering the first chapter provides for the even flow of following chapters.

This flashback exercise makes use of outlining skills. To help students, page numbers reference where outlining information can be found.

Flashback Development

Name_____

Directions: To understand how the author develops her introduction by using the flashback, complete the following outline by adding details from Chapter 1.

I. Wilderness Home Descriptions

A. tree home - _____ - p. 3

B. fireplace - _____ - p. 3

C. chimney - _____ - p. 3

D. ventilation knotholes - _____ - p. 3

E. lamp - _____ - p. 4

F. food supplies - _____ - p. 4

G. animal companions -

1. _____ - p. 4

2. _____ - p. 5

II. Flashback Description after December Snowstorm

A. _____ - p. 5

B. _____ - p. 5

III. Flashback Description of Narrator's New York Home

A. _____ - p. 8

B. _____ - p. 8

IV. Flashback Explanation of <u>Why</u> the Narrator Chose to Build his Home in the Catskills

A. _____ - p. 8

B. _____ - p. 8, 9

"IN WHICH I Get Started on This Venture"

Student Directives

1. List the possessions Sam had when he left New York.

2. Describe Sam's transportation from New York to the Catskill Mountains.

3. Describe that first night in the Catskills.

4. Discuss Sam's search that first morning—what he learned about tinder.

Vocabulary

venture (n) an action or plan involving chance, risk, or danger

tinder a material that burns easily and can be used as kindling

congregate to come together into a group or crowd

Summary

Sam Gribley (we don't learn his first name until the end of this chapter) detailed the few possessions he took when he left home. These included an ax, some flint, steel, and some tinder. In order to get to the Catskills, Sam hitched a ride from a truck driver. He described his first cold, lonely, frightening night in the Catskills. After finally succeeding in catching trout for his dinner, Sam told about his futile attempt to get a fire burning. He went to bed hungry, making yet another mistake by camping on the windiest side of the mountain. In the morning Sam set out to find some help. Fortunately, he found a house with an old man (Bill) inside who taught him how to keep tinder glowing by adding fine dry needles one by one—all the while blowing lightly, steadily, and evenly. Making fire, Sam discovered, is a vital skill for conquering the Catskills.

"THE MANNER IN WHICH I Find Gribley's Farm"

Student Directives

1. Describe Sam's feelings about making fire.

2. Review Sam's frustration in finding the Gribley farm at Delhi.

3. Tell about Sam's research at the library with Miss Turner and the disclosure of his plan.

4. Relate Sam's note to Bill.

5. Describe Sam's reaction to the first meal he prepared in the wilderness.

Vocabulary

strode   took very long steps

lolled   reclined in a lazy manner

combustible   capable of being burned

Summary

After telling Bill good-by, Sam knew he now had the power to conquer the Catskills—he could make fire. Sam hitched rides to Delhi but was frustrated in his attempt to locate the family farm. He researched maps and histories of the area at the Delhi library where he met Miss Turner, the librarian. Sam disclosed his plan to Miss Turner, explaining that he planned to live off the land on his great-grandfather's farm. Miss Turner was amazed but offered to help by providing books on plants and animals. After locating the farm, Sam cooked his own catfish and wrote Bill a note about his fire-building success. In the months to come, Sam would learn to cook better, but he would never enjoy a meal as much as his first meal in the Catskills.

"IN WHICH I Find Many Useful Plants"

Student Directives

1. Describe the warbler migration.

2. Relate how Sam learned what to eat.

3. Describe Sam's first breakfast in the Catskills.

4. Tell the value of hickory trees for Sam.

5. Discuss locating the ruined foundation of Gribley farm.

6. Describe Sam's discovery of the hemlock forest.

Vocabulary

migration   the act of moving from one country, place, or locality to another

edible   fit or safe to be eaten

mussels   freshwater mollusk with hinged double shell

implements   articles intended for use in work

Summary

When Sam awoke after his first morning in the Catskills, he saw birds everywhere and concluded that they must be the warbler migration. Sam had read that he should watch the birds and animals, especially raccoons, in order to learn which plants are edible. Sam discovered that it really does hurt to be hungry, so he hurriedly collected almost a peck of mussels and cooked them for his first wilderness breakfast. After discovering hickory trees, which would provide him with nuts and salt, Sam found the ruined foundation of the Gribley house. The marsh on this property provided him with cattail tubers and arrow-leaf—both good starchy foods. Sam's most exciting discovery, however, was the ancient gigantic hemlocks growing in the hemlock forest. Standing before the largest and most kingly tree, Sam suddenly had an idea.

"THIS IS ABOUT The Old, Old Tree"

Student Directives

1. Discuss Sam's need for a house that could not be seen.

2. Review Sam's decision to dig out a giant hemlock tree.

3. Describe Sam's food gathering and cooking.

4. Tell about Sam's decision to burn out the tree's cavity.

5. Relate how Sam learned the value of buckets.

Vocabulary

remote   out-of-the-way

primitive   of early times; of long ago

ravine   deep narrow gorge eroded by water

vague   not clearly defined or understood

Summary

Sam knew he would need a home that could not easily be seen, since many people vacation in the Catskills each summer. Circling the great hemlock tree, Sam decided to dig out its rotting inner cavity for his home. He became discouraged, though, because of the time and effort it took to gather his food. Sam ate the dogtooth violet bulbs, spring beauty flowers, and dandelions. He even boiled crow eggs in a skunk cabbage leaf. Since digging out the hemlock proved to be an endless task, Sam decided to use fire to speed the process. Sam discovered water from a spring, but since he had no bucket, he had no way to take the water back to the tree. Sam had never before appreciated the importance of buckets.

Elements of a Narrative

When an author creates a novel, a movie, or a television script, he or she must carefully plan a number of elements, which include: characters, setting, and plot. Simply stated, *somebody* has to be *somewhere* doing *something*. The author's story has merit if the characters are believable, engaging, and well developed. The setting(s) must be accurately described so that the reader can create a mental picture of it in his or her own mind. Specific details are vital in the development of a narrative; details make the story "come alive" for the reader.

Possibly the most complex narrative element is the plot. To develop the plot, the author must carefully plan a sequence of events which will hold the reader's or viewer's interest throughout the book, movie, or TV show. The author must concentrate only on the important aspects of the story so that it doesn't drag on endlessly. Additionally, the events must present a problem which the central character must resolve—either happily or unhappily.

Throughout the introductory chapters or scenes, the author must make these three elements—characters, setting, and plot— clear to the reader or viewer. Using the introductory chapters as a guide, complete the following "Elements of a Narrative Outline" from *My Side of the Mountain*.

Elements of a Narrative Outline

Name _____

Directions: Analyze the three basic elements of a narrative from your reading thus far in *My Side of the Mountain*. Complete the following outline for your analysis.

Main Character *(somebody)*   Describe the kind of person the main character is.

A. _____

_____

B. _____

_____

C. _____

_____

Setting *(somewhere)*   Describe the setting where the story unfolds.

A. Where: _____

_____

B. When: _____

_____

Plot *(something)*   From your reading so far, predict how the plot (a series of events) will be developed.

A. _____

_____

B. _____

_____

C. _____

_____

D. _____

TEST

My Side
of the
Mountain

Chapters 1-5, Page 1

Name _____

Multiple Choice

Directions:

Circle the letter of the
correct answer.

1. Sam Gribley decided to run away from home because...
   A. he had a disagreement with his parents.
   B. he wanted to live with his grandfather.
   C. his New York apartment was very crowded.

2. Sam's biggest problem on his first night in the mountains was...
   A. his fear of wild animals.
   B. his inability to get a fire started.
   C. his inability to find food.

3. When Sam awoke after his first night in the Catskills, he ...
   A. went to toward the road and found a house.
   B. stopped to get a ride from a truck driver.
   C. hiked to town so he could call home.

4. Bill helped Sam by teaching him...
   A. how to cook fish.
   B. how to keep the tinder glowing while adding twigs.
   C. how to find edible plants.

5. Miss Turner, the librarian at Delhi, helped Sam by...
   A. cooking a meal for Sam.
   B. introducing him to a man who lived in the woods.
   C. finding the maps and histories of the Gribley farm.

6. When it came to finding food, Sam discovered that...
   A. food from the wilderness was healthier than food from New York City.
   B. searching for food and cooking it was a time-consuming, never-ending process.
   C. he liked natural foods better than store-bought food.

Name _____

7. During the early December blizzard, Sam was...

A. cold, hungry, and frightened.

B. wishing that he had never left home.

C. warm, well fed, but trapped in his tree house for several days.

8. Sam knew that he had conquered the Catskills once he...

A. learned how to make a fire.

B. learned how to catch fish.

C. found the giant hemlock tree.

9. Sam had learned about the Gribley farm in the Catskills from...

A. his grandfather.

B. his father.

C. his mother.

10. Sam decided to build his hemlock house by...

A. chopping the tree down.

B. burning out its cavity.

C. building a tree fort in its boughs.

Vocabulary

Directions:

Fill in the blank with

the correct word.

inspired	combustible	implements
venture	migration	remote
congregate	edible	vague
	strode	

1. _____ took very long steps

2. _____ capable of being burned

3. _____ the act of moving from one country, place, or locality to another

4. _____   an undertaking involving chance,
                        risk, or danger

5. _____   not clearly understood

6. _____   given the spirit to act

7. _____   fit or safe to be eaten

8. _____   articles intended for use in work

9. _____   out-of-the-way

10. _____   to come together in a group or crowd

Essay Questions

Directions:

Answer in complete

sentences.

1. Tell two mistakes that Sam made on his first night sleeping
   out in the Catskills.

   A. _____

   B. _____

2. Explain how the author, Jean Craighead George, uses the
   flashback technique to introduce *My Side of the Mountain* .

   _____

   _____

   _____

3. Tell why it was so important for Sam to find a home that
   could not easily be seen.

   _____

   _____

   _____

"IN WHICH I Meet One of My Own Kind and Have a Terrible Time Getting Away"

Student Directives

1. Describe Sam's feelings after completing his house.

2. Tell about Sam's bed and food.

3. Discuss Sam's encounter with the little old lady.

4. Relate Sam's decision to trap a falcon.

Vocabulary

puckered   drew together into folds or wrinkles

escorted   went along with; accompanied as a protector

wiry   slender, yet strong and muscular

Summary

Sam felt very satisfied with himself after completing his hemlock house. He set about making himself a bed frame from ash tree slats. With the coming of summer, Sam's diet improved; he feasted on frogs' legs, turtles, an occasional rabbit, and cattail roots, which taste like potatoes if they are cooked long enough. One day Sam was startled by the appearance of a little old lady who had come to pick strawberries in the Catskills. Sam reluctantly helped her pick some of his precious strawberries. Although Sam enjoyed her conversation, hearing a human voice was difficult to get used to. While walking the little old lady home, Sam spotted a peregrine falcon and decided that he needed to capture one and train it for hunting.

"The King's Provider"

Student Directives

1. Discuss Sam's visit with Miss Turner at the library.

2. Relate Sam's experiences with trout fishing.

3. Describe Sam's capture of the nestling falcon.

4. Discuss Sam's feelings for Frightful.

Vocabulary

tubers	short, fleshy, usually underground stems
exertion	the act of pushing oneself into action vigorously
thrashing	moving or stirring about violently

Summary

Sam went to see Miss Turner at the library to learn about hawks and falcons. In addition to getting the information on falcons, Miss Turner gave him a much needed haircut. On his way to look for the falcon's nest, Sam went trout fishing, which is easy if the fish are hungry. Sam knew they were hungry that evening because the creek was swirling, and the minnows were jumping out of the water. Once he spotted the mother falcon, Sam followed it to its nest and took the largest nestling. The mother falcon attacked Sam. He placed the fuzzy little body under his sweater and slid down the ledge on the seat of his pants. He had to move quickly to escape. Sam immediately loved the nestling falcon, which he named Frightful.

"A BRIEF ACCOUNT OF What I Did About the First Man Who Was After Me"

Student Directives

1. Discuss Sam's reaction to the forester.

2. Relate Sam's conclusion regarding the forester's visit to Sam's camp.

3. Tell how Sam began to train Frightful.

Vocabulary

savory   pleasing to the taste or smell

resolved   reached a decision about

jesses   short straps fastened around the leg of the falcon

Summary

Sam sensed another human in the woods and discovered the fire warden, who had probably seen smoke from Sam's fires. While waiting for the fire warden to leave, Sam dressed down a trapped rabbit from its snare and gave savory bites of it to Frightful. Sam couldn't cook the rabbit over the smoky fire because he didn't want to alert the warden, so he made rabbit soup in an old tin can he had found, seasoning his soup with wild garlic and jack-in-the-pulpit roots. Lying down on an improvised bed of boughs, Sam resolved to keep a cleaner camp in the future. He repeatedly stroked Frightful because he had read that this would make her training easier. Sam went to bed dreaming of hunting expeditions he would make with Frightful.

"IN WHICH I Learn to Season My Food"

Student Directives

1. Describe how Sam met The Baron Weasel and his reaction to the animal.

2. Tell why Sam needed a deer.

3. Describe how Sam made salt.

4. Describe Sam's bed.

Vocabulary

berated   scolded forcefully

harassing   disturbing persistently, tormenting

device   a piece of equipment or machinery to serve a special purpose

residue   whatever remains after a part is taken, separated, or lost

Summary

At dawn, Sam checked his box trap and discovered that he had trapped an angry, scolding weasel. Sam was amazed at the weasel's bravery as the furious animal screamed and jumped on him. After a time, the weasel climbed down and marched off in a stately manner. Sam named the weasel "The Baron," and the two began a wonderful but harassing friendship. Sam knew that he needed to capture a deer so he could make a door for the hemlock tree, tethers for Frightful, and a blanket for himself. After the fire warden left, Sam went home and attempted to make salt from the residue of boiled hickory sticks. To Sam's delight, the thick black substance tasted just like salt, so he knew he would be able to flavor his food. Sam finished his bed made of ash slats and set to planning a way to capture a deer.

"How a Door Came to Me"

1. Relate The Baron Weasel's warning to Sam.

2. Tell how Sam outwitted the hunter and got a deer.

3. Review how earthworms made Sam smile.

Vocabulary

loping	moving or running with bounding steps
provoke	to anger or enrage
poaching	trespassing on another's land to steal game

Summary

Early one morning Sam was smoking the extra fish he had caught when The Baron Weasel alerted Sam to danger. A hunter was poaching in the woods and had shot a deer. Reaching the dead animal before the hunter did, Sam realized that the deer was just what he had been needing, so he dragged the deer's carcass into the woods. He then covered it with hemlock boughs and returned to his tree house. During that time, Sam had to keep stroking Frightful so she wouldn't cry out and alert the poacher. After a frightening morning, Sam was able to redeem his prize, and that night he feasted on venison steak. Sam was later amused by the "pops" of the earthworms as they came to the ground's surface. Sam felt that this was one of the nicest things he had learned in the woods.

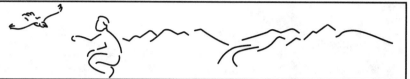
Name _____

Multiple Choice

Directions:

Circle the letter of the

correct answer.

1. When Sam met the little old lady picking strawberries, he...
   A. was glad because he wanted somone to talk to.
   B. invited her into his hemlock house.
   C. was annoyed because she was picking the best strawberries.

2. With the coming of summer, Sam's diet...
   A. consisted of nuts and berries.
   B. included no meat because the heat spoiled it.
   C. improved a great deal.

3. When Sam spotted the peregrine falcon, he decided that...
   A. he needed to capture one to train it to hunt for him.
   B. he needed a pet.
   C. it would be impossible to train the bird.

4. Sam was worried about removing the falcon nestling from its nest because...
   A. he did not know how to care for it.
   B. he was afraid that the mother falcon would attack him.
   C. he thought the bird would prove useless to him.

5. When Sam spotted the fire warden in the woods, Sam knew that the warden...
   A. had probably read about Sam in the newspaper.
   B. was just making a routine check.
   C. had probably spotted smoke from one of Sam's fires.

6. Sam spent a lot of time stroking Frightful because...
   A. her feathers were very soft.
   B. he had read that falcons repeatedly stroked were easy to train.
   C. Sam was bored in the wilderness.

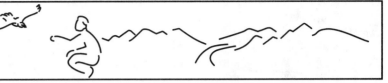

7. Sam first met The Baron Weasel when...

A. they met by chance in the woods.

B. the weasel invaded Sam's hemlock.

C. Sam captured the weasel in one of his box traps.

8. Sam was surprised at The Baron Weasel's reaction to him because...

A. the weasel showed no fear of Sam.

B. the weasel was smarter than the other animals Sam had attempted to capture.

C. the weasel bit Sam.

9. When Sam caught extra fish, he had to...

A. throw them back into the stream because he could not use them.

B. learn to smoke them until they were dry.

C. give them to the animals to eat.

10. Sam was finally able to get his first deer by...

A. setting a trap and capturing it.

B. dragging away the carcass of a deer that was shot by a poacher.

C. killing one by spearing it.

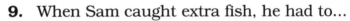

wiry	savory	harass
tubers	jesses	device
exertion	resolved	residue
	berated	

Vocabulary

Directions:

Fill in the blank with the correct word.

1. _____   scolded forcefully

2. _____   short, fleshy, usually underground stems

3. _____   pleasing to the taste or smell

4. _____   a piece of equipment or machinery to serve a special purpose

5. _____   to disturb persistently; torment

6. _____   the act of putting oneself into action

7. _____   short straps fastened around the leg of a falcon and attached to a leash

8. _____   slender, yet strong and muscular

9. _____   reached a decision

10. _____   whatever remains after a part is taken, separated, or lost

---

Essay Questions

Directions:

Answer in complete

sentences.

1. Give two facts about the falcon that Sam learned from his research at the Delhi Library.

    A. _____

    B. _____

2. Tell how The Baron Weasel differed from other animals that Sam had encountered in the woods.

    _____

    _____

    _____

3. Describe the process by which Sam was able to obtain salt to flavor his food.

    _____

    _____

    _____

"IN WHICH Frightful Learns Her ABC's"

Student Directives

1. Describe how Sam prepared the deer for tanning.

2. Tell how Sam used all parts of the deer.

3. Relate how The Baron Weasel tricked Sam while he was scouting for deer.

Vocabulary

steeped   soaked in water or other liquid

vessel   a hollow container for holding liquid or other contents

tethered   fastened by a rope or chain

personable pleasing in appearance or manner

Summary

Sam spent his free time preparing the deer for tanning. For this project Sam needed to get tannic acid from oak trees. First, Sam burned out an oak stump to use as a bucket. Then he steeped the deerskin for about five days in the stump filled with oak chips and water. After much work, Sam made a deerskin door for his tree home. All parts of the deer were used: the meat for food, the skin for a door and Frightful's jesses, and some bones for spearheads. Sam's city clothes had become threadbare, so he needed to trap another deer so that he could make a deerskin suit. The Baron Weasel played a trick on Sam while Sam was stalking deer near one of his traps. The Baron Weasel jumped at Sam and nipped him on the ankle, causing him to cry out and to frighten away the deer.

"IN WHICH Frightful Learns Her ABC's"

Student Directives

1. Tell why Sam enjoyed the summer.

2. Relate the threat that hikers and vacationers posed for Sam.

3. Describe how The Baron Weasel helped Sam.

4. Tell how Sam captured another deer.

5. Discuss how Sam trained Frightful to the lure.

Vocabulary

abundance   a large quantity

tedious   long and tiresome

maneuvers   skillful moves

hover   to hang fluttering or suspended in the air

Summary

Sam spent the summer gathering food and training Frightful to the lure. He burned out another tree to store his stockpile of nuts and acorns. Sam was not the only one enjoying the summer in the Catskills. Hikers and vacationers often passed by Sam's tree home on their way to the gorge. One morning Sam heard a shrill scream from an animal, most likely a deer that had been caught in one of his traps. He wanted to investigate, but he stopped when he heard hikers tramping around his camp. The fiery Baron Weasel came to Sam's rescue and chased the hikers away. When Sam was finally able to claim the deer, he set about making himself a deerskin suit. Sam's training with Frightful began to pay off. She was becoming trained to the lure; she would catch meat that was tied to a piece of wood covered with hide and feathers. When it was thrown into the air, Frightful would bring it back to earth. Soon after the training sessions, she was catching her own prey.

Outlining

Use after Chapter 11.

Outlining is an essential skill for organizing your thoughts and learning new material. Below is an article written about the uses Sam Gribley had for deer. Like the American Indians before him, Sam used as much of the deer as possible. Read the article and consult the Topics List to complete the outline.

Remember that outlines are divided into main topics, sub-topics, and supporting information. Outlines provide you with a shortened, well-organized structure for recalling and studying new information.

Sam's Uses of Deer

Sam Gribley needed deer to survive winter in the wilderness. After accidentally finding a deer carcass, Sam set out to find as many uses for it as possible. Sam used the deerskin to make a door for his hemlock tree, to make jesses and leashes out of deerskin strips for Frightful, and to make a deerskin suit for himself.

In order to use the deerskin, Sam had to follow several preparatory steps: (1) He scraped the fur off the hide. (2) He steeped the deerskin in tannic acid from oak chips and water after devising a bucket from an oak stump. (3) He dried the hide. (4) He softened the hide by chewing, rubbing, twisting, and jumping on it. After following all these steps, the first deer hide was ready to use.

Another part of the deer Sam used was the meat. Since he couldn't eat all of the meat right away, Sam smoked the meat and stored it for later use.

Like the American Indians, Sam also used the bones of the deer. One tool Sam made from deer bones was a spearhead, which he used to catch frogs so he could enjoy frog-legs dinners. Sam's procedure for making the spearhead was as follows: (1) He sharpened two bone points. (2) He strapped the points to the end of a long stick. (3) He fashioned the tool like a fork with one point on each side. Sam also used bones to make needles for sewing.

Sam was very proud of his accomplishment in finding so many uses for deer.

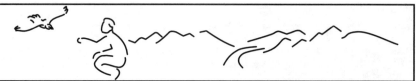

Outlining

Name _____

Directions: An incomplete outline for "Sam's Uses of Deer" is given in the left column. Choose from the Topics List in the right column to complete the outline. Parts of the outline have been properly placed for you.

Sam's Uses of Deer	**Topics List** Choose from:
I. Skin	
A. Uses of Deerskin	
1. _____	Dry hide
2. _____	Door—hemlock tree
3. _____	Strips—jesses and leashes (Frightful)
B. Preparation of Deerskin	Soften hide
1. _____	Scrape fur off hide
2. _____	Deerskin suit
3. _____	Steep in tannic acid
4. _____	
II. Meat	
A. _____	Smoke and store
B. _____	Eat fresh
III. Bones	
A. Uses of Bones	
1. _____	Sharpen bone points
2. _____	Needles—sewing
B. Making Spearheads	Make tool—like a fork
1. _____	Spearheads—catching frogs
2. _____	Attach to stick
3. _____	

"IN WHICH I Find a Real Live Man"

Student Directives

1. Relate how Sam met Jessie Coon James.

2. Describe the police sirens and Sam's encounter with the man sleeping by his tree home.

3. Tell how Bando helped Sam.

4. Relate Bando's farewell promise to Sam.

5. Describe Sam's reunion with his animal friends.

Vocabulary

vengeance great force or violence

preen to trim or dress with a beak, as a bird does its feathers

furtively in a sly, shifty manner

characteristic typical of an individual's behavior

Summary

Sam befriended another animal while taking his daily bath in the cold spring waters. Jessie Coon James was a scraggly, cross-eyed, orphaned raccoon that Sam took home and fed. Jessie proved valuable to Sam in digging for mussels. One day Sam heard the piercing sound of a police siren and wondered about the cause of the search. As Sam approached his tree house, he noticed a sleeping man by his home. Even though Sam assumed the man was an outlaw, he befriended him. Sam called his friend Bando and was surprised to learn that he was a college English professor who had gotten lost in the Catskills. Bando stayed with Sam for a week or more and helped him by building a raft, preparing blueberry jam, making pottery dishes from clay, and making a willow whistle for entertainment. Bando promised Sam that he would return at Christmastime. Alone again, Sam reunited with his animal friends—Frightful, The Baron Weasel, and Jessie Coon James.

Sequencing

Name _____

Event 1: Sam hitchhikes to Catskills.

_____

Event 2: _____

_____

Event 3: Miss Turner helps locate farm.

_____

Event 4: _____

_____

Event 5: _____

_____

Event 6: _____

_____

Event 7: _____

_____

Event 8: _____

_____

Event 9: Baron Weasel caught in Sam's

trap. _____

Event 10: _____

_____

Event 11: _____

_____

Event 12: _____

_____

Directions:

Using the timeline provided, sequence the following events from Chapters 1-12. Three events have been done for you.

- Sam meets strawberry lady.
- Sam hitchhikes to Catskills.
- Sam discovers deer carcass.
- Miss Turner helps locate farm.
- Sam captures falcon nestling.
- Sam creates oak stump bucket.
- Baron Weasel caught in Sam's trap.
- Sam discovers fire warden.
- Bill explains about fire.
- Sam discovers hemlock tree.
- Sam makes deerskin door.
- Sam burns out tree's cavity.

Cause and Effect

Name _____

Directions: On the left is a list of causes. On the right is a list of effects. Match the correct effect with its cause by placing the correct letter in the blank.

A **Cause** produces a result	An **Effect** results from a cause
1. Because Sam's New York apartment was too crowded, ____	A. it will bite at anything.
2. Sam added twigs too rapidly to the fire, so ____	B. Sam noticed a man wearing a forester's uniform coming to check on fires.
3. When the fish's stomach is empty, ____	C. he built a smoking rack of hard hickory sticks rather than soft pine sticks.
4. Since female falcons are the hunters and larger than the males, ____	D. he realized that earthworms make a slight popping sound as they come to the surface.
5. Because Sam hasn't heard a human voice in months, ____	E. he kept stroking her until she became hypnotized.
6. When he continued making fires during a dry spell, ____	F. Sam picked the largest nestling from the falcon's nest.
7. Because he didn't want a smoky fire, ____	G. he asks the little old lady to speak slowly.
8. Since Sam's first batch of smoked fish was ruined by black smoke, ____	H. Sam used only the driest wood to build his fire.
9. Sam needed to keep Frightful quiet, so ____	I. he decided to live off his great-grandfather's land.
10.When Sam heard a soft "pop, pop" noise from the grass, ____	J. he couldn't get his first fire going.

Comparison and Contrast

Name_____

Sam's Hero

Sam Gribley loved nature. He loved it enough to live his life totally enveloped in a natural setting. Sam needed to feel the wind and rain. He needed to feel the grass growing beneath his feet. Sam needed to watch the squirrels scampering up trees as branches swayed in the breeze. He needed to smell the moist richness of the earth and to awake to the birds' serenades. Sam needed to get as close to nature as he possibly could.

Sam Gribley was not the first person to love nature so deeply. Sam's hero was a man named Henry David Thoreau, who lived about 100 years before Sam was born. From your reading, you know that Bando immediately understood that Sam was imitating the lifestyle of this famous naturalist. As a result, Bando always referred to Sam as "Thoreau."

In fact, Bando was amazed at the similarities between Sam Gribley and Henry David Thoreau. We remember Bando remarking, "Am I dreaming? I go to sleep by a campfire that looked like it was built by a boy scout, and I awaken in the middle of the eighteenth century...Thoreau, you are quite wonderful."

Who was Henry David Thoreau, and why did Bando immediately connect Sam with him? Henry David Thoreau was a naturalist who was born in Concord, Massachusetts, in the early 1800s. Growing up, Thoreau was different from other boys his age. He did not enjoy sports, games, or parties, but spent much of his time alone, wandering in the woods. Thoreau was a scholarly boy who loved reading and knew about a great many things. People who knew him well would comment, "He always *was* odd."

Thoreau did well in school and eventually went on to study at Harvard College. While at Harvard, Thoreau discovered the writings of Ralph Waldo Emerson, also a Harvard graduate. Later, Thoreau and Emerson became close friends and shared ideas. They both composed essays and poems. They also gave lectures.

In 1845, when Thoreau was twenty-seven years old, he wanted to do serious writing—a book. Since he needed a quiet place to think and write, Emerson gave Thoreau permisssion to build a small hut on woodsy land he owned by Walden Pond. Thoreau's house was only a bit larger than a toolshed, but he lived there over two years, studying nature, thinking, and writing.

During his time at Walden Pond, Thoreau ate the potatoes and corn he raised, the fish he caught, and the wild plants he found. When he wanted companionship, he walked to town and had dinner with family or friends.

Comparison and Contrast, Page 2

Name_____

Thoreau had visitors as well as his animal neighbors to keep him company. One of Thoreau's favorite wild visitors was a loon that played tricks on him.

Thoreau was very happy at Walden Pond. He loved watching the snow fall and seeing the earth come back to life in spring. The story of Thoreau's two years at Walden Pond was entitled simply *Walden*. Although the book did not sell particularly well during his lifetime, its sales increased steadily after his death. Thoreau died a happy man at the age of forty-four from tuberculosis. He had never needed success or money during his lifetime, but only the opportunity to live life as he wanted. About his own life, Thoreau wrote, "My life has been the poem I would have writ." Today, many people regard Thoreau as a visionary—one who understood nature and our relationship with all living things.

Directions: Using your book and the article "Sam's Hero," make a Comparison/Contrast Chart about Sam Gribley and Henry David Thoreau.

Similarities		Differences	
Sam	**Thoreau**	**Sam**	**Thoreau**

"IN WHICH The Autumn Provides Food and Loneliness"

Student Directives

1. Tell how Sam enjoyed autumn and prepared for winter.

2. Describe the changes in The Baron Weasel's coat.

3. Relate Sam's fears about winter.

4. Describe Sam's fireplace.

5. Tell how Sam learned about ventilation.

Vocabulary

boldly	in a daring manner
harsh	severe, not gentle
verge (n)	edge, brink
sensation	a physical feeling like pain or cold

Summary

Autumn blazed into the Catskills and Sam felt the world was wonderful. He busily gathered bulbs, tubers, and roots for winter food; he also smoked fish and rabbit. The Baron Weasel began to shed his summer coat in preparation for a white winter mantle. Sam realized that if he was to stay in the Catskills, he needed a fireplace. After much trial and error, he finally constructed his fireplace from clay mixed with dry grass. Sam learned a nearly fatal lesson when he made his first fire in the new fireplace. After the fire had burned for a while, Frightful's eyes became glassy and she toppled off her bedpost. The fireplace had used up all the oxygen. Sam opened the deer flap to get her some water and the night air revived her. Sam then realized that he had to ventilate his tree house, or they both would die.

"IN WHICH We All Learn About Halloween"

Student Directives

1. Describe Sam's food-gathering strategies for winter.

2. Discuss Sam's preparation for his Halloween party.

3. Describe the antics of the "guests" who attended Sam's party, including his least favorite guest.

4. Relate how Sam finally got rid of the unwelcome guests.

Vocabulary

resented	felt or showed displeasure as from an insult
ferocity	the quality of wild appearance or action
precaution	a measure taken beforehand to secure good results
eerie	weird, strange; inspiring fear

Summary

With the coming of autumn, Sam and the wilderness creatures searched for food to store for the winter months. Sam realized that Halloween was approaching, so he decided to throw a Halloween party for the animals. He made piles of food for his guests: cracked nuts, smoked rabbit, crayfish, and apples. This was an invitation for the squirrels, foxes, raccoons, and birds to enjoy a feast. The first night was uneventful, but the second night brought some unruly, unwelcome guests. Not only did the animals eat Sam's party food, but two raccoons also invaded the tree house. A skunk sprayed Sam, and a bat flew into his house. Sam finally got rid of his unwelcome guests by growling and snarling at the animals, showing them that he was the biggest and strongest of them all.

"IN WHICH I Find Out What to Do with Hunters"

Student Directives

1. Relate Sam's reaction to the coming of hunting season.

2. Tell how Sam was able to get another deer from a hunter.

3. Discuss how Sam used his deerskins.

Vocabulary

moral   teaching a lesson to be learned from a story or experience

swarm   a great number of things or people, usually in motion

preserve   to prepare food to keep it from spoiling

Summary

Sam was awakened by a gunshot in early November and realized that hunting season had begun. Like the animals, Sam decided to stay hidden in his house. One morning Sam was dangerously close to a hunter and climbed a tree to escape his notice. Watching the hunter track his deer, Sam saw the deer jump a stone fence and fall dead, probably from a heart attack. The hunter was unable to find the animal, so Sam was able to capture his third deer. Before the season had ended, Sam was able to get two more deer in the same manner. The air temperature was now cold enough to preserve the venison, so Sam didn't smoke the meat. He made himself a deerskin blanket and a deerskin jacket with pouches for storage.

Multiple Choice

Directions:

Circle the letter of the

correct answer.

1. When Sam needed to soak his deer hide, he got a vessel big enough for the job by...
   A. finding an iron bucket someone had left in the gorge.
   B. burning out a hole in an old oak stump.
   C. checking with Miss Turner at the Delhi library.

2. Sam trained Frightful to come when he whistled by...
   A. jerking slightly on her leash.
   B. petting her to coax her to come.
   C. feeding her each time she would come to his whistle.

3. With the coming of summer, Sam worried about...
   A. the heat spoiling his meat.
   B. hikers and vacationers spotting his tree house.
   C. The Baron Weasel stealing his food.

4. Jessie C. James was the name Sam gave to...
   A. a skunk who had invaded his hemlock tree.
   B. a weasel Sam had captured in his box trap.
   C. a young raccoon who looked like he had been orphaned by his mother.

5. When Sam encountered a man in the woods just after hearing police sirens, Sam decided...
   A. not to hide from the man, but fed him instead.
   B. to turn the man over to the police.
   C. to hide in the woods until the man left.

6. When Sam attempted to guess Bando's line of work, Bando reacted by...
   A. getting angry with Sam for calling him an outlaw.
   B. laughing at Sam.
   C. stealing Sam's food and deerskins.

7. When Bando left Sam to return to the city, he promised Sam that...

A. he would never forget Sam.

B. he would write a book about their wilderness adventure.

C. he would return to visit Sam at Christmastime.

8. With the coming of winter, Sam noticed that The Baron Weasel's fur was looking moldy. Sam concluded that...

A. The Baron Weasel was sick.

B. The Baron Weasel was growing a white mantle for winter.

C. The Baron Weasel was not keeping his fur clean.

9. The first time Sam used his clay fireplace to heat his hemlock tree house, he realized that...

A. he needed to ventilate his tree or he and Frightful would die.

B. the fireplace was too large for his tree house.

C. he would not be able to chop enough wood to keep his fire going during the winter.

10. Sam was able to frighten the animals after the Halloween party by...

A. throwing large rocks at the animals.

B. showing the animals that might makes right and that he was the biggest and oldest of them all.

C. dousing them with water.

Vocabulary

Directions:

Fill in the blank with

the correct word.

steeped	hover	ferocity
personable	vengeance	eerie
tedious	characteristic	abundance
	boldly	

1. _____   in a daring manner

2. _____   soaked in water or other liquid

3. _____   to hang fluttering or suspended in air

4. _____   weird, strange; inspiring fear

5. _____   long and tiresome

6. _____   pleasing in appearance or manner

7. _____   quality of wild appearance or action

8. _____   great force or violence

9. _____   typical of an individual's behavior or appearance.

10. _____   a large quantity

Essay Questions

Directions:

Answer in complete

sentences.

1. Explain why Sam initially thought that Bando was an outlaw.

_____

_____

_____

2. Tell three ways Bando improved Sam's life in the woods.

_____

_____

_____

3. Tell one way The Baron Weasel proved helpful to Sam and one way he hindered Sam.

_____

_____

4. Using specific details, describe the mess the animals made at Sam's Halloween party.

_____

_____

_____

"IN WHICH Trouble Begins"

Student Directives

1. Describe Sam's winter clothes.

2. Discuss Sam's encounter with the boy at the drugstore.

3. Tell what important job Sam had neglected to do.

Vocabulary

dignity   a quality or state of being worthy, honored, or respected

plumage   the large showy feathers of a bird

assured   self-confident

conspicuous attracting attention

Summary

By the end of November, Sam was dressed in his new winter suit made entirely of deerskin and lined with rabbit fur. He had made mittens and squirrel-lined moccasins. Sam was very proud of his woodland wardrobe. Because he was lonely, Sam made a sudden decision to go into town. While browsing through the magazine rack, Sam struck up a conversation with a boy his own age who Sam called "Mr. Jacket." The boy was amazed by Sam's appearance and referred to him as "Daniel Boone." Sam invited Mr. Jacket to Gribley's farm to join him in some research. When Sam returned home, he realized that he needed to stock up on wood for winter.

"IN WHICH I Pile Up Wood and Go on with Winter"

Student Directives

1. Discuss Sam's fears about winter.

2. Relate how Sam made his woodpile.

3. Describe Sam's winter activities with Frightful.

Vocabulary

quarry   an animal or bird hunted as game or prey

originated   brought into existence; created

Summary

   As winter approached, Sam became more frightened and nervously stockpiled wood to ease his fears. He began stocking the wood an arm's length from his home so that he would be able to reach it in the event of a storm. When the fierce winter storm finally broke, Sam was almost relieved because he was well prepared. Once the storm had ended, Sam found his mountain home a white, glistening wonderland. To entertain themselves, Sam and Frightful went ice fishing and scavenged for plants beneath the snow. Frightful still hunted pheasant and rabbit. At home, Sam experimented with cooking, wrote on birch bark, and made new things out of deer hide. Both Sam and Frightful enjoyed their winter evenings.

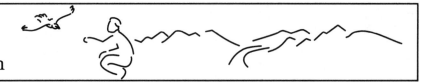

Categorizing: Wilderness Foods, Page 1

Name_____

Directions: Categorizing is an important skill for organizing and recalling information. Using the list of Wilderness Foods, organize Sam's food into the appropriate categories.

dandelion greens
beechnuts
May apples
rabbit
cattail roots
strawberries
teaberry leaves
wild onions
wild carrots

water lily buds
pennyroyal
arrow-leaf tubers
catfish
hickory nuts
honey locust beans
mussels
blueberries
dogtooth violet bulbs

trout
sassafras roots (tea)
walnuts
venison
hawthorn berries
wild garlic
raspberries
liver (from rabbit)
jack-in-the-pulpit roots
acorns

Meats

1. _____

2. _____

3. _____

Fish

1. _____

2. _____

3. _____

Starchy Foods

1. _____

2. _____

3. _____

Fruits/Berries

1. _____

2. _____

3. _____

4. _____

5. _____

Vegetables

1. _____

2. _____

3. _____

Greens

1. _____

2. _____

Categorizing: Wilderness Foods, page 2   Name_____

Nuts/Acorns	Drinks	Foods for Flavor
1. _____	1. _____	1. _____
2. _____	2. _____	2. _____
3. _____		3. _____
4. _____		

Throughout *My Side of the Mountain*, Sam vividly describes many meals he prepared. If you were able to be Sam's guest for dinner, what meal would you like him to prepare?

Your Wilderness Dinner Menu

_____

_____

_____

_____

_____

_____

_____

"IN WHICH I Learn About Birds and People"

Student Directives

1. Discuss Sam's reactions to the winter months.

2. Tell Sam's names for the woodland chickadees.

3. Describe Sam's Christmas reunion with Bando.

4. Relate how people knew Sam was living in the Catskills.

Vocabulary

portico   roof supported by columns, forming a porch

adorned   heightened in appearance with ornaments

ingenious   very clever and inventive

wistfully   in a sadly thoughtful manner

Summary

Sam thoroughly enjoyed winter in the Catskills. He was pleasantly surprised that he did not become lonely and found that winter was just as exciting as summer. Sam enjoyed the woodland chickadees and compared them to his neighbors on Third Avenue: Mr. Bracket, Mrs. O'Brien, Mrs. Callaway, and Mrs. Federio. As Christmas approached, Sam was worried that Bando might not return for his visit. Despite his apprehension, Sam prepared a Christmas feast for Bando and made him some presents. Bando arrived on Christmas Eve with a group of newspaper clippings about Sam. Both Sam and Bando were delighted to spend Christmas together.

"IN WHICH I Learn About Birds and People"

Student Directives

1. Tell about Sam's surprise Christmas guest.

2. Relate how Sam's father was able to find him.

3. Describe Sam's Christmas feast.

Vocabulary

sired	fathered
rendition	a particular interpretation, as of a song
sanguine	cheerful; hopeful
reluctantly	showing hesitation or unwillingness

Summary

On Christmas Day, Sam received a surprise visitor—his father. After a joyful reunion, Sam's father explained that he was able to find Sam's whereabouts from reading newspaper articles about Sam and from questioning Mrs. Fielder, the strawberry lady. Bando, Sam's father, and Sam celebrated a memorable Christmas. They feasted on onion soup, venison steaks, sassafras tea, mashed cattail tubers, and honey locust beans mixed with hickory nuts. They all played Christmas carols on flutes that Bando fashioned from hollow reeds. Bando reluctantly left a few days after Christmas, but Sam's father stayed on until New Year's.

"IN WHICH I Have a Good Look at Winter and Find Spring in the Snow"

Student Directives

1. Describe winter after Christmas was over.

2. Tell how Sam entertained himself during the winter months.

3. Describe the hemlock forest after the ice storm.

4. Relate how Sam learned about vitamin C.

5. Discuss the signs of spring in the mountains.

Vocabulary

barometer   an instrument that measures the pressure of the atmosphere to determine probable weather changes

retreat   the act of going away, especially from something difficult, dangerous, or disagreeable

concoction   a combination of ingredients

resilient   having the ability to recover or spring back

Summary

After Christmas was over, winter weather became fierce. To entertain himself, Sam slept, ate, played his reed whistle, and talked to Frightful. Sam was very healthy and never even had a cold. After plowing through many snowdrifts, Sam devised a pair of snowshoes made of ash slats and deer-hide strips. One damp and drizzly day, the temperature suddenly dropped, and the entire hemlock forest froze. Ice on the ground and trees was inches thick. Trees began to crack and splinter, and Sam feared that his hemlock might shatter too. After the weather warmed, the forest was strewn with shattered tree limbs and the bodies of birds and animals that had frozen. Sam was shocked but realized that this process had been going on for thousands of years. Toward the end of January, Sam began to tire easily; his bones ached, and he got a nosebleed. He wondered if he was experiencing a vitamin deficiency. Sam naturally began craving liver, which cured his problem. Later Sam discovered that liver is rich in vitamin C. Then, signs of spring began emerging. Deer began foraging again and the great horned owls laid their eggs in snowy tree cavities.

"MORE ABOUT The Spring in the Winter and the Beginning of My Story's End"

Student Directives

1. Discuss more signs of spring.

2. Describe Sam's encounter with Matt Spell.

3. Relate Sam's agreement with Matt.

4. Review Sam's imaginary forum about Matt's visit.

Vocabulary

momentum increased speed in the unfolding of events

conceded granted as a right or privilege

forum a meeting or program involving discussion

Summary

Winter was slowly giving way to spring in the mountains. Insects appeared in the snow, birds built nests, raccoons mated, foxes called to their lifelong mates, ferns unrolled, and sap ran in the maple trees. One day Sam was startled to hear a boy his own age ask him, "You're the wild boy, aren't you?" After regaining his composure, Sam denied it. Matt Spell explained that he worked after school on a New York newspaper and that he had come to investigate the persistent rumors about a boy living alone in the wilderness. Sam skillfully led Matt on a confusing trip through the forest. Sam then told Matt a fabricated story about the whereabouts of the "wild boy." Sam's trickery failed, however, and Matt told Sam the details of his article about Sam's life. Sam made an arrangement with Matt. In exchange for altering the details of Sam's whereabouts, Sam agreed to let Matt join him for spring vacation. That night, Sam held an imaginary forum with his father, Bando, Matt, and Frightful, discussing the advisability of Matt's upcoming visit.

What Do You Think About Conflict? Name _____

Use after Chapter 20.

Toward the end of the story, Sam began to crave the company of humans more and more. During this time, Sam experienced conflicting feelings. On the one hand, Sam wanted to continue his natural, solitary life in the Catskills. Sam was immensely proud that he had conquered the wilderness, and he did not want to trade his accomplishment for human company. On the other hand, Sam naturally craved the company and conversation of humans like himself.

1. Give at least two examples from the story which demonstrate that Sam deliberately sought out human companionship.

   _____

   _____

   _____

   _____

   _____

   _____

   _____

2. Have you ever experienced a time when your feelings were in conflict? A time when you wanted two conflicting things? Give one example from your own life when you experienced conflict.

   _____

   _____

   _____

   _____

   _____

   _____

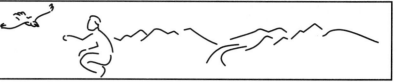
Name _____

Multiple Choice

Directions:

Circle the letter of the correct answer.

1. When Sam met "Mr. Jacket," the boy in the drugstore, Sam decided that...
   A. he didn't like the boy because Mr. Jacket had made fun of his clothes.
   B. he did like Mr. Jacket even though they had never even had a fight.
   C. he should come to town more often.

2. With the coming of winter, Sam knew he needed...
   A. more wood for fuel.
   B. more companionship.
   C. more activities to amuse himself.

3. Sam felt that the winter evenings in the tree house were...
   A. long, lonely, and boring.
   B. happy because The Baron Weasel kept him company.
   C. busy with cooking, writing, and making things for Frightful.

4. Sam enjoyed watching the birds during winter because...
   A. they were beautiful.
   B. they reminded him of his neighbors on Third Avenue in New York.
   C. he was training them as pets.

5. When Christmas Eve arrived, Sam felt that...
   A. he wanted to go home to be with his family.
   B. Bando had forgotten his promise or was too busy to come.
   C. he would rather spend Christmas Day alone with Frightful.

6. When Bando left Sam after his Christmas visit, Bando...
   A. went reluctantly because he envied Sam's way of life.
   B. was happy to leave because the hemlock tree was crowded.
   C. told Sam he was leaving his teaching job at the university.

7. Sam's dad felt that Sam...

  A. should return home because his mother missed him.

  B. had done very well living in the wilderness.

  C. looked unhealthy.

8. Sam noticed that birds kept warm in freezing weather by...

  A. flying around a great deal.

  B. hiding in a tree's cavity.

  C. fluffing their feathers.

9. Sam knew he had a vitamin deficiency because...

  A. his skin color turned yellow.

  B. he became tired easily, and he got nosebleeds.

  C. his vision became blurred.

10. Matt Spell was a boy who...

  A. Sam had met at the drugstore in Delhi.

  B. had been Sam's friend in New York.

  C. worked for a newspaper and wanted to investigate the "wild boy" rumors.

Vocabulary

Directions:

Fill in the blank with

the correct word.

plumage	wistful	concoction
conspicious	sanguine	resilient
forum	barometer	conceded
	ingenious	

1. _____ sadly thoughtful

2. _____ the large showy feathers of a bird

3. _____ granted as a right or privilege

4. _____ cheerful, hopeful

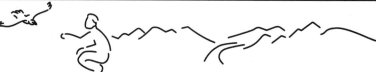
5. _____   having the ability to recover

6. _____   very clever and inventive

7. _____   a combination of ingredients

8. _____   attracting attention

9. _____   an instrument that measures atmospheric pressure to determine possible weather changes

10. _____   a meeting or program involving discussion

Essay Questions

Directions:

Answer in complete sentences.

1. Sam was happy in the wilderness, but he sometimes got lonely. Give three examples from any previous chapter which show that Sam wanted to talk to humans.

   A. _____

   B. _____

   C. _____

2. Sam did not dread winter as he had feared. Tell some of Sam's winter activities.

   _____

   _____

   _____

3. Describe Sam's Christmas in the Catskills.

   _____

   _____

   _____

4. Why did Sam describe the nuthatch as a weather barometer?

   _____

   _____

"IN WHICH I Cooperate with the Ending"

Student Directives

1. Discuss how the animals changed when spring arrived.

2. Relate how Sam's diet and habits changed in spring.

3. Tell about Sam's encounter with Aaron.

4. Discuss Sam's frequent visitors.

Vocabulary

sagely   wisely

pondered   considered carefully

Summary

The animals changed their habits once spring appeared. They no longer paid attention to Sam—not even The Baron Weasel or Jessie Coon James. The chickadees sang alone, not in a group, because winter was no more. By April, Sam's diet became more varied and he resumed his daily baths in the spring. One day Sam met a man named Aaron in the woods. Aaron was a songwriter and Sam sang him his "cold water song." Several days later, Matt joined Sam for his spring break. Toward the end of the week, Bando joined the boys, and they decided to make a guest house out of one of the other trees. Sam realized that he no longer was a runaway. After Matt and Bando left, Sam was joined by "Mr Jacket," whose real name was Tom Sidler. Both Tom and Bando visited Sam often, and Sam felt sad that his wilderness way of life had changed. Aaron also came back and wrote more songs. Sadly realizing that he was no longer the "wild boy of the Catskills," Sam asked Bando to bring him some blue jeans and a shirt on his next visit.

Character Development

Use after
Chapter 21.

Sam Gribley was a remarkable teenage boy. Leaving the safety and security of his New York home, Sam daringly set out to create a home of his own in the Catskill wilderness. To be successful in his adventure, Sam first needed to explore the depths of his own character. Sam knew that in the wilderness he could depend on only one person—Sam Gribley.

Jean Craighead George masterfully develops Sam's character through Sam's thoughts and actions. Sam's success in achieving his dream was almost entirely dependent on his own strength of character. The reader comes to know Sam Gribley as a young man whose virtues, or character strengths, enable him to overcome obstacles that would have overwhelmed a lesser person.

Good literature, like *My Side of the Mountain*, serves not only to entertain and educate us, but also to enrich us spiritually. In analyzing Sam's character, not only do we learn about his character development, but we are also given examples of how we can strive to conduct our own lives. Like Sam Gribley, we must develop our own strength of character.

The Discovering Literature Series focuses on ten character virtues:

Responsibility	Friendship
Courage	Persistence
Compassion	Hard Work
Loyalty	Self-discipline
Honesty	Faith

My Side
of the
Mountain

Character Development, Page 1

Name_____

Directions: Sam Gribley portrays a strong, responsible character in *My Side of the Mountain.* Give examples from the novel to illustrate the virtues listed below.

Responsibility

_____

_____

_____

_____

Courage

_____

_____

_____

_____

Friendship

_____

_____

_____

_____

Persistence

_____

_____

_____

_____

_____

Character Development, Page 2

Name_____

Hard Work
_____
_____
_____
_____
_____

Self-discipline
_____
_____
_____
_____
_____

Can you think of other qualities that Sam possessed?

_____ : _____
_____
_____
_____
_____

_____ : _____
_____
_____
_____
_____

Which of Sam's virtues would you like to imitate? Why?

_____
_____
_____
_____
_____

"IN WHICH The City Comes to Me"

Student Directives

1. Relate what occurrences left Sam with a heavy heart.

2. Relate Sam's conflict when his dad arrived.

3. Tell why Sam jumped for joy.

4. Discuss Sam's mother's plan.

Vocabulary

hordes	crowds of people
self-sufficient	able to take care of oneself without outside help
inferring	arriving at a conclusion from facts
editorials	articles in a newspaper or magazine that give the opinion of its editors or publishers

Summary

Many photographers and reporters were visiting the Catskills to photograph and interview Sam. Sam's heart was heavy as he realized that he no longer had the freedom to live his wilderness existence. Later in June, Sam's dad came to visit him. At first Sam hesitated, wondering if he should run away so that he could conquer some as-yet-unexplored territory, but his desire to see his dad overcame those thoughts. Soon Sam jumped for joy as he realized that his dad had brought the entire family with him. After an uproarious reunion, Sam's dad explained that the family had all come to live in the Catskills. That night Sam ate his mother's fried chicken for dinner and humorously commented, "Chicken is good, it tastes like chicken." The next day his father began erecting a house. When Sam protested, his mother gently reminded him, "That's how it is until you are eighteen, Sam." And that ended it.

What Do You Think About Reality?

Name _____

Use after
Chapter 22.

Sam Gribley's story is fiction. Even though the author, Jean Craighead George, supplies the reader with a wealth of technical information about wilderness survival, the story *My Side of the Mountain* is a product of her imagination. With the information you have learned from your reading, do you think that a boy like Sam would really have been able to survive alone in the wilderness? Do you think it likely that he would have returned home after a few days or weeks? Do you think that Sam likely would have encountered situations he couldn't control? Do you think, in reality, that the police or forest rangers would have discovered him?

Continue writing on
additional paper as
needed.

Tell what you think would really have happened to Sam if he tried to survive the wilderness alone. Give reasons for your answer.

_____

_____

_____

_____

_____

_____

_____

_____

_____

_____

_____

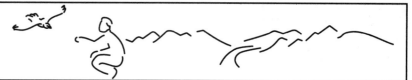
A Presentation

Name _____

Directions:

Choose one of the following suggestions. Develop it so that you can make a presentation to your class.

1. Write a letter to Sam Gribley telling him your reactions to his successes in wilderness survival.

2. Pretend that you are an editor of a New York newspaper. Compose an editorial comment about Sam's parents' responsibility to provide food and shelter for him. You will remember that the newspaper editorials made Sam's mother feel that she was not meeting her motherly responsibilities.

3. Pretend that you are an investigative reporter sent to interview Sam about his life in the Catskills. Write an article for your paper about Sam. (Be sure to answer all of the reporter questions: Who? What? Where? When? Why? and How?)

4. Pretend that you are a hiker lost in the Catskill Mountains and you encounter Sam in the wilderness. Write a dialogue between you and Sam that could have taken place while you were lost. (Remember that a dialogue is composed entirely of direct quotes.)

5. Pretend that you are Sam Gribley and you have been invited to give a talk about wilderness survival to your class. Dress up like Sam. (You may want to use brown mailing paper and/or brown grocery bags to construct your "deerskin" suit.) Give a presentation to your class about some important elements of wilderness survival.

6. Research and make a chart (with diagrams) of edible plants that could be safely eaten in the wilderness.

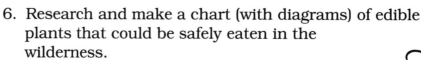

7. Write a short narrative of your own (fact or fiction) and tell about a wilderness or camping experience.

8. Pretend that you are Sam and you are keeping a daily journal of your experiences with wilderness survival. Write a number of journal entries. (You may want to write your entries on "birch bark" the way Sam did. Use brown wrapping paper or construction paper.)

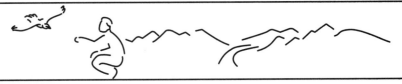
Plot Development, Page 1

Authors must plan for three major elements—characters, setting, and plot—when creating a story. Of the three narrative elements, plot is usually the most difficult to develop.

In every well-developed plot, the central character has a problem, or conflict, to overcome. The central problem can be a conflict between two people, between a character and the society in which she or he lives, between a character and nature, or it could even be a conflict within the main character. Whatever the conflict, the main character works through his or her problem throughout the novel or script. In doing so, the main character encounters a series of minor problems, or difficulties; however, these are all directed at resolving the major conflict.

The structure of a plot can be compared to climbing a mountain. At the base of the mountain, the reader is introduced to the main characters and to the setting. The story develops and the reader is presented with a major problem to be overcome. All the while, the reader is steadily climbing the mountain until he or she reaches the peak, where the action reaches a high point or climax. As soon as the climax has been reached, the action falls rapidly—just as a mountain climber would when rushing down the back side of a mountain. Once the action falls, the reader sees the central character resolve her or his problem.

Choose between two plot activities.

Choice A—Plot Organization Map

The Plot Organization Map (on the following page) graphically illustrates how the plot is developed. Using the following Rising Action topics and Falling Action topics, plot the novel's events sequentially. Then fill in the characters, setting, problem, and resolution.

Duplicate the Plot Organization Map on oversize paper for ease of student use.

Rising Action

- Sam befriends The Baron Weasel.
- Sam traps deer.
- Sam's decision.
- Sam enjoys winter.
- Sam builds his home.
- Sam captures/trains Frightful.
- Sam meets Mr. Jacket.
- Sam conquers fire.
- Sam's whereabouts becomes known.
- Sam helps Bando.

Falling Action

- Sam's family arrives.
- Visitors flock to see Sam.

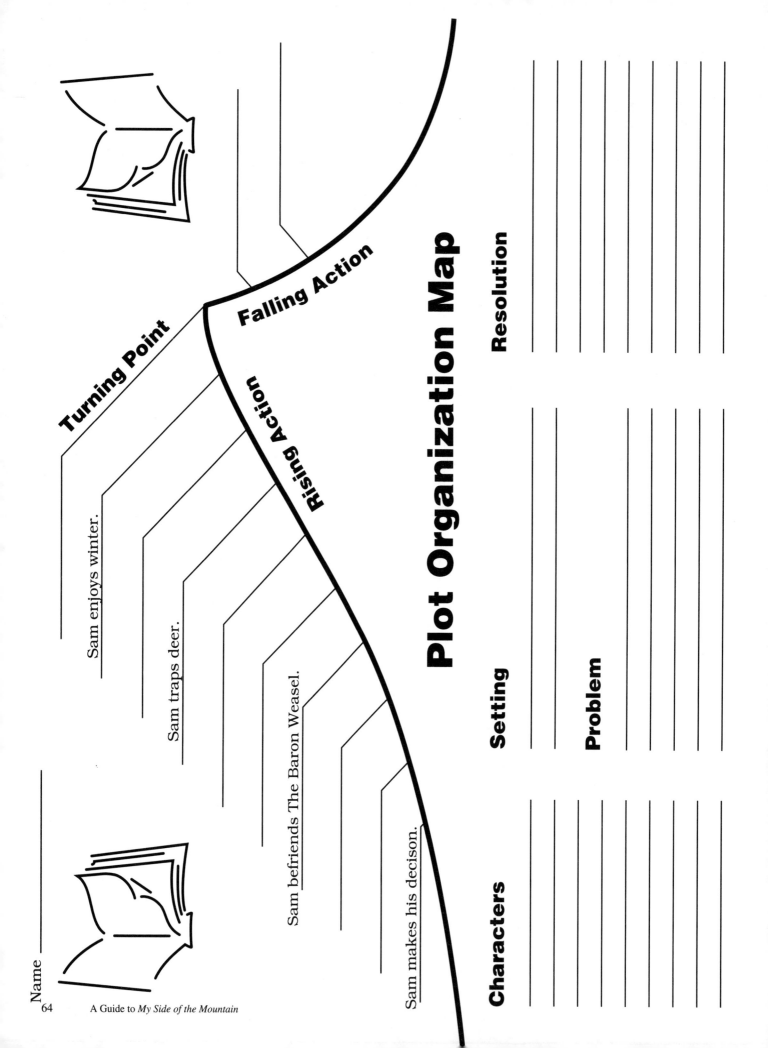

Plot Organization Map

Turning Point

Falling Action

Rising Action

Sam enjoys winter.

Sam traps deer.

Sam befriends The Baron Weasel.

Sam makes his decison.

Resolution

Setting

Problem

Characters

Plot Development, Page 2

Choice B—Story Mountain Art Project

The Story Mountain Art Project allows students to visually construct the plot of *My Side of the Mountain*: the introductory elements, the rising action, the turning point, the falling action, and the resolution.

Students, working in groups, construct a papier mâché mountain, paint it, and decorate it with grass and stones. The plot is analyzed with major events written on stick-em notes placed strategically on the completed mountain.

<u>Materials for Mountains</u>
Newspapers
1 or 2 buckets
Water
Cardboard box tops
3 - 2 oz. jars of art paste
Wide paint brushes
Imitation grass (from craft shop or plastic Easter basket
                grass)
Small stones
Glue

<u>Materials for Flags</u>
Stick-em notes (8 to 10 per mountain)
Toothpicks
Clay or sticky tack

Plot Development, Page 3

Directions

1. Before mixing the art paste, you may want to discuss the irregular shape of mountains. Show any pictures available. Practice wrinkling the dry newspaper into irregular shapes so students will not produce flattened mountains.

2. Mix art paste according to directions. Dip the newspaper into the paste and form mountains, making as many folds, creases, and irregularities as possible.

3. Allow mountains to dry. (This can take a few days, depending upon how much paste the students use.)

4. Paint the mountains with brown tempura.

5. Decorate with grass and stones.

6. Write out the major points of the story's plot.

7. Copy plot points onto stick-em notes. Attach notes to toothpicks. Insert notes with toothpicks into clay or sticky tack. Place on mountain. Make sure the students place the climax at the highest point on the mountain, with the falling action and resolution on the shorter side.

CHAPTER SUMMARY & VOCABULARY	My Side of the Mountain	

Chapter Title _____ Name _____

Chapter Summary: _____

_____

_____

_____

_____

_____

_____

_____

_____

_____

_____

_____

_____

_____

_____

Chapter Vocabulary:

1. _____

_____

2. _____

_____

3. _____

_____

4. _____

_____

NAME: _____

My Side of the Mountain

Flashback Development. Page 11.

I. Wilderness Home Description

   A. tree home - hemlock tree six feet in diameter - p. 3

   B. fireplace - made of clay and stones; knee-high - p. 3

   C. chimney - leads smoke out - p. 3

   D. ventilation knotholes - let fresh air in - p. 3

   E. lamp - deer fat poured into turtle shell with strip of city trousers for a wick - p. 4

   F. food supplies - kept in wooden pockets in wall of the tree - p. 4

   G. animal companions -

      1. The Baron Weasel - p. 4

      2. Frightful, a trained falcon - p. 5

II. Flashback Description after December Snow-storm

   A. White, clean, shining snow - p. 5

   B. Blue, blue sky - p. 5

III. Flashback Description of Narrator's New York Home

   A. New York City apartment - p. 8

   B. 11 people - Dad, Mom, four sisters, five brothers - p. 8

IV. Flashback Explanation of <u>Why</u> the Narrator Chose to Build his Home in the Catskills

   A. Very crowded apartment - p. 8

   B. Heard stories about Great-grandfather Gribley's farm from his father - p. 8, 9

      Accept reasonable answers.

Skill Page: Elements of a Narrative. Page 17.

Main Character

A. The main character left the security of his New York home to carve out a life in the Catskill wilderness. He is adventuresome.

B. The main character knows how to find solutions for his problems. He is resourceful.

C. The main character is not afraid to live by himself in the Catskill wilderness. He is brave.

Setting

A. Where: The story takes place in the Catskill Mountains of upstate New York.

B. When: The story takes place sometime in the mid-1900s.

Plot

A. A teenage boy from New York City leaves his home to create a home in the Catskill wilderness.

B. The boy encounters many problems such as finding food and shelter.

C. The boy is ultimately successful; that is, he does make a home for himself in the mountains.

   Accept reasonable answers.

Test: Chapters 1-5. Pages 18-20.

Multiple Choice

1. C	6. B
2. B	7. C
3. A	8. A
4. B	9. B
5. C	10. B

Vocabulary

1. strode	6. inspired
2. combustible	7. edible
3. migration	8. implements
4. venture	9. remote
5. vague	10. congregate

Test: Chapters 1-5. (Con't.)

Essay Questions

1. A. Sam failed to get a fire going. P. 16-17

   B. Sam camped on the windiest side of the mountain. P. 17

2. Accept any reasonable answer.

3. Sam did not want to be caught living in the wilderness because the authorities would send him home. P. 29

Test: Chapters 6-10. Pages 26-28.

Multiple Choice

1. C	6. B
2. C	7. C
3. A	8. A
4. B	9. B
5. C	10. B

Vocabulary

1. berated	6. exertion
2. tubers	7. jesses
3. savory	8. wiry
4. device	9. resolved
5. harass	10. residue

Essay Questions

1. •Female nestlings are larger. •Females are the hunters. •Falcons are easier to train if you stroke them. P. 44 & 49.

2. The Baron Weasel was the bravest animal that Sam had encountered. He showed no fear and jumped and screamed at Sam for capturing him. P. 51

3. Sam boiled hickory sticks dry, which left a salty residue. P. 53

Accept reasonable answers.

Skill Page: Outlining. Page 31.

Sam's Uses of Deer

I. Skin
   A. Uses of Deerskin
      1. Door—hemlock tree
      2. Strips—jesses and leashes (Frightful)
      3. Deerskin suit
   B. Preparation of Deerskin
      1. Scrape fur off hide
      2. Steep in tannic acid
      3. Dry hide
      4. Soften hide
II. Meat
   A. Eat fresh
   B. Smoke and store
III. Bones
   A. Uses of Bones
      1. Spearheads—catching frogs
      2. Needles-sewing
   B. Making Spearheads
      1. Sharpen bone points
      2. Attach to stick
      3. Make tool like a fork

Skill Page: Sequencing. Page 34.

Event 1:   Sam hitchhikes to Catskills.

Event 2:   Bill explains about fire.

Event 3:   Miss Turner helps locate farm.

Event 4:   Sam discovers hemlock tree.

Event 5:   Sam burns out tree's cavity.

Event 6:   Sam meets strawberry lady.

Event 7:   Sam captures falcon nestling.

Event 8:   Sam discovers fire warden.

Event 9:   Baron Weasel caught in Sam's trap.

Event 10:   Sam discovers deer carcass.

Event 11:   Sam creates oak stump bucket.

Event 12:   Sam makes deerskin door.

Skill Page: Cause and Effect. Page 35.

1. I	6. B
2. J	7. H
3. A	8. C
4. F	9. E
5. G	10. D

Test: Chapters 11-15. Pages 41-43.

Multiple Choice

1. B	6. B
2. C	7. C
3. B	8. B
4. C	9. A
5. A	10. B

Vocabulary

1. boldly	6. personable
2. steeped	7. ferocity
3. hover	8. vengeance
4. eerie	9. characteristic
5. tedious	10. abundance

Essay Questions

1. Sam heard police sirens down the road and saw patrol cars, so he assumed the man was an outlaw. P. 72-73

2. Bando helped Sam build a raft. He made blueberry jam. He made pottery dishes. P. 82-83

3. The Baron Weasel helped Sam by frightening away two hikers who had wandered into Sam's camp. The Baron Weasel hindered Sam by nipping at Sam's ankle so that he cried out and frightened the deer away. P. 61-62, 64-65.

4. They had strewn Sam's acorns and beechnuts over his floor and bed. A skunk sprayed Sam. The raccoons played with Sam's dried fish and venison. P. 99-100

Accept reasonable answers.

Skill Page—Categorizing: Wilderness Foods. Pages 46-47.

Meats
1. rabbit
2. venison
3. liver (from rabbit)

Fish
1. catfish
2. mussels
3. trout

Starchy Foods
1. cattail roots
2. arrow-leaf tubers
3. dogtooth violet bulbs

Fruits/Berries
1. May apples
2. hawthorn berries
3. raspberries
4. blueberries
5. strawberries

Vegetables
1. wild onions
2. wild carrots
3. honey locust beans

Greens
1. dandelion greens
2. teaberry leaves

Nuts/Acorns
1. hickory nuts
2. walnuts
3. beechnuts
4. acorns

Drinks
1. sassafras roots (tea)
2. pennyroyal

Foods for Flavor
1. wild garlic
2. water lily buds
3. jack-in-the-pulpit roots

Test: Chapters 16-20. Pages 53-55.

Multiple Choice

1. B	6. A
2. A	7. B
3. C	8. C
4. B	9. B
5. B	10. C

Vocabulary

1. wistful	6. ingenious
2. plumage	7. concoction
3. conceded	8. conspicuous
4. sanguine	9. barometer
5. resilient	10. forum

Essay Questions

1. A. Sam enjoyed hearing the local and world news from the strawberry lady. P. 39
   B. Sam wanted to talk to the man he thought was an outlaw. P. 73
   C. Sam went to the Delhi drugstore to meet people. P. 108

2. Sam ice fished and dug for plants buried under the snow. P. 114 Sam cooked new meals and wrote on birch bark. P. 114-115 Sam made snowshoes and walked on them. P. 132

3. Sam prepared a Christmas feast for himself and Bando. He made Bando moccasins and a hat from deer hide. Sam was surprised by a visit from his father. They played Christmas carols on reed flutes Bando had made. P. 118-128

4. A barometer shows possible weather changes. When the nuthatch holed up in its tree, Sam knew that bad weather was approaching. P. 133-134

Accept reasonable answers.

Skill Page: Character Development. Pages 57-59.

Possible examples to support virtues.

Responsibility:

In the wilderness, Sam Gribley could count on only one person—himself. If he hadn't assumed the responsibility of providing for his own food, clothing, and shelter, he would have perished.

Courage:

It took a great deal of personal courage for Sam to carve out a home for himself in the wilderness. He had to battle not only the elements but loneliness.

Friendship:

Sam gave friendship to each person he encountered during his year-long stay in the Catskills. He helped Mrs. Fielder, the strawberry lady, pick her strawberries. He provided food and shelter for Bando. He befriended The Baron Weasel and Jessie Coon James. He invited Matt Spell, the newspaper reporter, to visit him. He helped Aaron write his songs. He invited Mr. Jacket (Tom Sidler) to visit him.

Persistence:

Sam never gave up his dream of carving out a home in the wilderness even though, at times, he was cold, hungry, lonely, and frightened.

Hard Work:

In the beginning, Sam had to work constantly to provide for himself. Even the simplest tasks were time consuming: finding food, starting a fire, burning out the hemlock tree, making a bed, capturing and training Frightful, making traps, skinning and cleaning his catches, making a fireplace. It was all very hard work.

Self-discipline:

Sam had to make sure that he kept working constantly—especially in preparation for winter. If Sam had spent all his time playing during the warm weather, he would never have had the necessary food, clothing, or wood to get through the winter.

Culminating Project: Plot Development. Page 63-66.

Name _____Key_____

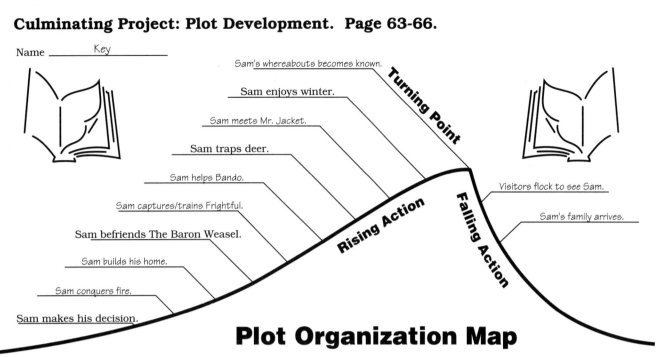

Sam's whereabouts becomes known.

Sam enjoys winter.

Sam meets Mr. Jacket.

Sam traps deer.

Sam helps Bando.

Sam captures/trains Frightful.

Sam befriends The Baron Weasel.

Sam builds his home.

Sam conquers fire.

Sam makes his decision.

Turning Point

Rising Action

Falling Action

Visitors flock to see Sam.

Sam's family arrives.

Plot Organization Map

Characters
Sam Gribley

Mom

Dad

Miss Turner

Bando

Mr. Jacket (Tom Sidler)

Matt Spell

Setting
Grandfather Gribley's farm—Catskill Mts., upstate NY

Problem
Sam Gribley runs away from crowded New York City apartment to live off the land on his great-grandfather's farm in the Catskill Mountains.

Resolution
Sam realizes that while he loves his wilderness home, he also craves human companionship. Little by-little, his story becomes known, and his family joins him in the Catskills.